EASTER
IS IT PAGAN?

By

Ralph Woodrow

A complete catalog of books and tapes may be obtained by contacting:

RALPH WOODROW
P. O. BOX 21
PALM SPRINGS, CA 92263-0021

Phone order line: (760) 323-9882
Fax: (760) 323-3982

*"The path of the just is as the shining light,
that shineth more and more
unto the perfect day"*
—*Proverbs 4:18.*

International Standard Book Number: 0-916938-16-6

Copyright © 1996
Second Printing 1998

Ralph Woodrow Evangelistic Association, Inc.
P.O. Box 21, Palm Springs, CA 92263-0021

Printed in the United States of America

INTRODUCTION

Growing up in church, I had known Easter as a victorious and joyous celebration of Christ's resurrection. More people attended church at this season than any other time of the year. It was while attending an Easter service that a man received Jesus Christ as his Savior, who later became my pastor. I had no reason to question there was anything wrong with Easter.

In time, however, I would read literature that targeted the observance of Easter as being "heathen idolatry," that it was "pagan to the core!" The very word "Easter," it was claimed, was the name of a pagan goddess! Easter was brought into the professing church by "Constantine" at the "Nicene Council"! A passage in Ezekiel was quoted to show that people who attend Easter sunrise services are worshipping the sun-god Baal! The 40 days of Lent, it was said, came right out of ancient Babylon! And Easter eggs and rabbits were abominable, vile, pagan, fertility symbols!

While never buying the whole package—I did not suppose Christians who celebrate Easter are worshipping Baal!—I did pass on some of the negatives in earlier editions of my book *Babylon Mystery Religion*. In time I would be quoted in many booklets, tracts, and articles dealing with the subject of paganism in Christianity, some of which promoted radical viewpoints.

Unfortunately, the anti-Easter teaching sometimes breeds a contempt and hostility, not only against the celebration of Easter, but also against those who celebrate it. It tends to reinforce an attitude in some—"The churches are all wrong anyhow!"

Let me hasten to say, if a custom or belief is indeed pagan, of course we do not want it! But what I have come to understand is this: We must proceed with caution about identifying something as "pagan" merely because a similar practice existed at some other time and place. Sometimes the "proofs" of paganism only have the *appearance* of being so. Bits and pieces of information taken from mythology cannot substitute for actual history. Incomplete information can lead to false conclusions. A few pieces of a puzzle, even though valid pieces, do not show the whole picture.

Within the pages that follow, I will share with you my studies which have caused me to *reconsider* the subject of Easter in a more positive light. I will try to present this information in ways that are strong enough to make the point, yet want to assure the reader that nothing is intended in an unkind or unfriendly way. I have Christian friends on both sides of this issue, friends that I regard highly!

In addition to this book, ***Easter, Is it Pagan?*** three other "reconsidered" books are also available: ***Christmas—Reconsidered***, ***"Three Days and Three Nights"—Reconsidered***, and ***The Babylon Connection?*** See page 57.

EASTER
IS IT PAGAN?

The celebration known as Easter is defined in *The Encyclopedia Britannica* as "the annual festival observed throughout Christendom in commemoration of the resurrection of Jesus Christ." *The World Book Encyclopedia* says: "Easter celebrates the return to life of Jesus Christ, the founder of Christianity, after His Crucifixion." Statements such as these are typical of what we would find in any encyclopedia.

Easter, for many Christians, is a time of rejoicing, victory, and joy as they celebrate the resurrection of Christ, knowing that because he lives, we can live also—forever!

But for others, Easter is looked on with suspicion. They do not believe it is a Christian celebration at all, that it should be totally rejected, that it is *pagan!*

One common objection is the word "Easter" itself. Dictionaries can be quoted to the effect that the word, in its original usage, was related to *Eostre,* a goddess of spring. This is based on a statement made by the Venerable Bede in the eighth century, which has been commonly echoed. But how reliable is this information? Who was the goddess Eostre? Do we know anything at all about her? Even the *Edda*, by the historian Snorri Sturluson (1178-1241), considered to be quite complete on the subject of mythology, fails to mention any goddess by this name.

The belief that "Easter" comes from the name of a pagan goddess is far from conclusive. *The World Book Encyclopedia* mentions several different viewpoints that are held by scholars. *The Encyclopedia of Religion* says: "The English name *Easter*...probably derives from *Eostur,* the Norse word for the spring season, and not from *Eostre,* the name of an Anglo-Saxon goddess."[1]

One writer sums it up this way: "Generations have been raised on the theory that the word 'Easter' came from pagan mythology. The Venerable Bede, an English historian and theologian of the eighth century, when the holiday first began to be called Easter, wrote that it was named for *Eostre,* an Anglo-Saxon goddess. This must have been conjecture on his part, because recent scholars can locate no reference to such a goddess in northern mythology.

"The German word *Ostern,* as well as its English equivalent, 'Easter,' is derived from the Norse *eostur, eastur,* or *ostara,* which meant 'the season of the growing sun,' 'the season of new birth.' A similar word, *ost* or "east," is used for the direction in which the sun rises. So it looks as if our English word for the spring holiday commemorating the Resurrection comes from the season *and not a pagan deity.*"[2]

But, for our present study, let's assume the word "Easter" was the name of a goddess—a pagan word. Would this necessarily mean the word is *still* pagan?

Or can words change in meaning and significance? Please consider the following six points:

1. Words commonly develop and change over a period of time, sometimes moving far away from their "original" meanings.[3]

An interesting example of this is provided by the word "tragedy." It comes from the Greek *tragos* (goat) and *ode* (song), meaning "goat-song"! It designated a ritual dance, with singing, in which one or more of the performers wore goatskins and played the part of a goat! Today we use the word "tragedy" in all kinds of circumstances—having nothing to do with a goat!

The word "nightmare" has nothing to do with a horse. It is based on an obsolete word, linked with witchcraft, meaning a female incubus—a demon that lies on persons in their sleep! But the word nightmare is now used to describe any bad dream. No one would limit it to its "original" meaning.

"Trivia" comes from the Latin *tri* (three) and *via* (road), a place where three roads meet, a place common to all roads, hence, commonplace, ordinary, insignificant. Today, we use the word trivia without the slightest thought about three roads!

The word "holiday" comes from "holy day," though for many people a holiday is not a holy day. It might be a holiday from school, a holiday from work, a day to get away and have a good time. The word no longer conveys a religious meaning.

French is called a *romance* language because it is based on Latin, the language of Rome. Consequently, narratives of love and adventure written in French were called "romances." In time, "romance" acquired a general meaning as we use it today—that emotional attraction between two people. It is now so far removed from its original linkage, many who use the word "romance" do not even realize the obvious: it is based on the word *Roman!*

We commonly speak of a couple going on their "honeymoon." But the word is based on a Hun tradition of a newly married couple drinking honeyed wine every night during the first month (moon) of their marriage. Today the word has acquired a different meaning, totally separate from the original custom on which it is based.

The word "bridal" is from Old English *bryd* (bride) and *ealu* (ale, ale-drinking). Today we might say: "Her bridal gown was of pure silk" or "The bridal party arrived at the church," usage that has nothing to do with whether anyone drinks ale or not!

"Mrs." is the normal, accepted title for a married woman. But it is only a shortened form of *mistress,* which is now commonly used in a different way. Today, if we say a man has a "mistress," no one would take this to mean his wife! His mistress would not be his Mrs.

There is nothing wrong with using "Mr." in front of a man's name; it is perfectly acceptable English. But if one wanted to argue against this title, he could point out that Mr. is only a shortened form of "master," and from this it could be further argued that Jesus said not to be called masters! (Matt. 23:10). So are we going to waste time preaching against the word "Mr."?

Those who insist that a word must always be understood in its *original* meaning, might have a problem with the word original! "Original," like the word "Orient," is based on *orior,* to rise, meaning the east, the direction of the rising *sun!* It would be foolish, of course, but some might even argue that the *original* meaning of "original" is pagan!

Whatever may have been the "original" meaning of Easter, proper word usage requires that we understand the word in the way it is used now.

2. Not only can a word move away from the significance of its original meaning, in time it can move upward, even from a negative or offensive meaning, to a proper and better meaning.

The word "travel" is an example of this. For thousands of years, travel was often difficult and torturous. Consequently, "travel" is just a variant of *travail!* Today, the word no longer conveys this negative meaning. To travel on a vacation, to travel and see the country, etc., has a pleasant ring to it.

Our word "pharmacy" is from the Greek *pharmakeia*—the word translated "witchcraft" in the New Testament—while a *pharmakon,* a pharmacist or druggist, was one who practiced "sorcery" (Strong's Concordance, 5331, 5332). Drugs were linked with the black arts, potions, etc. But today a pharmacy or drug store may sell all kinds of items, it is not a sorcery shop.

The word "consider" is common enough, but it comes from Latin *con* (thoroughly) and *sidus* (star). It was originally a word used in divination, meaning to deliberate on the positions of the stars. Now, it has acquired a meaning totally separate from divination, so that even our Biblical translators do not hesitate to say: *"Consider* the lilies of the field..." (Matt. 6:28).

In school we learned "spelling." This is good; but the word did not always have a good meaning. The Germanic peoples of the late Roman empire endowed letters with magical properties, so that "spelling" (from Old French *espeler*) was synonymous with casting *spells!* Imagine someone today saying, "I am not going to allow my child to take 'spelling' in school—its pagan!"

The word "pamphlet" seems innocent enough, but its origin was not lily white. *Pamphilus seu de Amore,* a best seller of the 12th century, was a pamphlet-sized love manual containing the story of an old woman who ran a house of prostitution. It was so popular that other similar-sized works became known as "pamphlets," based on the first word of this title!

A second year student in high school is called a "sophomore," a common designation, and with no negative tone today. But sophomore originally meant a wise *fool!* It is based on the Greek *sophos* (wise), plus *moros* (moron)!

The word "gymnasium" originally meant a place of *naked* exercise, based on the Greek practice of exercising in the nude. When the Greeks had control of Jerusalem, a gymnasium was built there for this purpose (1 Macc. 1:11-16). *Gymnos* is the Greek word translated "naked" in the New Testament (Heb. 4:13). But today the word gymnasium has acquired a general meaning, entirely separate from the word naked.

I know of churches that have built a "gym" for the purpose of getting young people off the streets, providing a wholesome Christian environment for sports and other activities. But for those who suppose a word must always be taken in its "original" meaning, a church with a gym could be accused of providing a place for naked exercise!

The word "testify" is used in courts and church services. But, as strange as it may sound, the word was originally linked with *testes* (testicles). When taking a solemn oath, a man would place his hand on this area (his or another's) as being representative of the life force. The practice, apparently widespread in ancient times, is mentioned several places in the Bible, the word "thigh" being used euphemistically (Gen. 24:2-4; 47:29).

What then? Is "testify" an inappropriate or vulgar word? Not at all, for by common usage it is far removed from its original meaning. A minister who calls on people to "testify" during a church service, is not telling them where to put their hands! Our translators use "testify" a number of places in the New Testament. Even the word "testament" (related to *testify*) is used to designate the Old Testament and New Testament of the Bible!

These are examples of words that, despite their original meaning, have now acquired a general and acceptable meaning. We believe that Easter is in this same category. If it was once linked with the worship of a pagan goddess, this obviously is no longer its meaning.

3. As strange as it may sound, even a word used *incorrectly* can, in time, acquire an established and acceptable meaning.

When Columbus supposed he had landed in a portion of India, he called the inhabitants "Indians." This was, of course, incorrect: Native Americans are not inhabitants of India! But by the time this error was discovered, the term Indian had become established and has remained.

The word "September" means *seven* (but is actually the ninth month), "October" means *eight* (but is actually the tenth month), "November" means *nine* (but is actually the eleventh month), and "December" means *ten* (but is actually the twelfth month). When the months July and August (named after the Caesars, Julius and Augustus) were inserted into the calendar, September, October, November, and December were all pushed ahead two months!

The word "ounce" comes from Latin *uncia,* a twelfth, because in Roman times a pound consisted of 12 ounces. Today, even though *we* figure a pound as 16 ounces, we still use the word "ounce" meaning twelfth!

"Quarantine" comes from *quarantina*, meaning 40. In earlier times, 40 days of isolation were imposed upon ships, persons, and goods arriving at a port when suspected of carrying a contagious disease. Today we still use the word quarantine, but without any linkage to the number 40.

The Romans added a column of figures from the bottom to the top, and then, at the top, wrote the total or *sum*. "Sum" is from the Latin *summus*, meaning highest, from which we get words like summit. *We* add a column of figures from top to bottom, and write the total at the bottom. Still we call it the *sum* (top)! We speak of summing *up*—as the Romans did—even though we have added *down* through a column of figures!

"Noon" comes from the Latin *nona hora,* the ninth hour, and originally corresponded with what we call 3 PM. Though we still use the word noon, it is obviously not the ninth hour today.

The word "matinee" is used to describe a performance of a play or movie in the afternoon—before a later evening performance. But the word can be traced to the French *matin,* which means *morning!*

In all of these instances, the word usage is *technically* incorrect. Yet, there is no misunderstanding, because in time these words have acquired established meanings.

Is the term Easter "incorrect"? If it is, like these examples, it is only incorrect in a technical sense. The overwhelming evidence for what it means now, totally outshines any ancient and obscure meaning! All encyclopedias say that Easter is the spring celebration of Christians in honor of the resurrection of Jesus Christ! Not one says it is the time when Christians honor Eostre. This would really be incorrect!

4. Because words can change in meaning, it is important that they be understood in the sense they are used at any given time.

Suppose someone wrote about a visit to New York: "We went to Coney Island and ate hot dogs." If a scholar were to read these words a few centuries later, unless he understood them as they were used *at the time they were written,* he might conclude that Coney Island was shaped like a cone, probably an extinct volcano; that it had an extremely hot climate; and the native people there ate dogs!

I once heard a preacher use as his text: "I will stand upon my watch" (Hab. 2:1). Several times he emphasized these words through the course of his message: *"I will stand upon my watch!"* The Old Testament figure here is that of a guard watching from a tower. But if one were to think of a "watch" in its present-day meaning—a *wrist watch* for keeping time—he might question why the preacher kept talking about standing on his watch!

Four hundred years ago, in a context of rings, earrings, bracelets, and bonnets, the King James translators used the word "muffler"—a long veil worn by women (Isa. 3:19). But today, we understand "muffler" as part of the exhaust system on a car. That was not, and could not have been, the meaning back then!

Unless Habakkuk had a wrist watch—and unless women owned automobiles at the time of Isaiah—it is quite clear that words like "watch" and "muffler" must be understood in the sense they were used *at the time.*

If a book written thousands of years ago described a spring festival called "Easter," it would be incorrect to force a present-day meaning on the word. It would need to be understood within the context of the time it was written. By the same token, if we are speaking of Easter as it is celebrated now, it is incorrect to give it some obscure and ancient meaning. Words must be understood within their proper time frame.

5. Many words we use are based on the names of pagan gods and goddesses. But because such words have acquired a general, non-pagan meaning, we need not refrain from using them.

We do not refrain from using the word "janitor," even though it comes from Janus, the Roman god of doors and gates. We do not refrain from using the word "cereal," even though it comes from Ceres, the goddess of grains. We do not refrain from using the word "panic," even though it comes from the god Pan who went about scaring people!

We do not refrain from calling a book of maps an "atlas," even though it comes from Atlas who was, in mythology, condemned to support the earth for eternity. We don't refrain from using the word "money," though it is said to come from Juno *Moneta,* a goddess to whose temple a Roman mint was attached.

We do not hesitate to call the central building of the United States government the "Capitol," even though the word comes from Jupiter Capitolinus, the temple of the god Jupiter which stood on Capitoline Hill in ancient Rome.

We do not refrain from using the word "cloth," even though Clotho, a daughter of Jupiter and Themis, was the goddess that spun the thread of life. We do not refrain from using the word "flower," even though Flora was the goddess of flowers. We do not refrain from using the word "ocean," even though Oceanus, son of Uranus, was the god of the sea.

We do not refrain from using the word "insomnia" (sleepless), even though Somnus was the god of sleep. He was the father of Morpheus, god of dreams, from whose name we obtain the word "morphine."

We do not refrain from using the word "echo," even though Echo was a mountain nymph whom Juno deprived of speech except when spoken to. Luke did not hesitate to use the Greek word *echos*—echo—when describing the reverberating "*sound [echos]* from heaven as of a rushing mighty wind" on the day of Pentecost (Acts 2:2).

We do not refrain from using the word "fury," even though the Furies were, in mythology, three hideous, winged female deities who went about punishing people and inflicting plagues.

We do not refrain from using the word "circle," even though some attempt to link it with Circe, a mythological sorceress who turned people into swine.

The "Muses" were the nine daughters of Zeus who presided over learning and the arts. From "Muses" we obtain our words *museum* and *music*. Does this make "museum" a bad word? Is it "pagan" to visit a museum? Should we preach against "music" because the word once had pagan linkage?

It is said that the word "hymn" is from Hymen, Greek god of marriage, a hymenal song being a wedding hymn. If so, would this mean we should refrain from singing hymns or that hymns honor the god Hymen?

We do not refrain from using the word "siren" —the shrill rise-and-fall sound of an ambulance, fire engine, or police car—even though it comes from the evil, mythological Sirens whose shrill singing lured sailors to shipwreck and death.

We do not refrain from using the word "thunder," even though it comes from *thunor*, related to Thor, the god of thunder, whose name also gives us Thursday, literally "Thor's Day"!

The Gospel writer Matthew did not refrain from using a Greek word that is translated "fair weather" (Matt. 16:2), even though it is linked with *Zeus,* the god of weather (Strong's Concordance, 2105, 2203). Doubtless it had become a common expression, without pagan significance, by the time he wrote.

Paul did not refrain from using the word "Corinth" (1 Cor. 1:2), even though the city took its name from *Corinthus,* who in Greek legend was a son of Marathon. He did not refrain from using the word "Ephesus" (Eph. 1:1), even though the name of this city, located on the Cayster River, was named after its legendary founder, *Ephesus,* son of the river-god Cayster.

We do not refrain from calling a South American river the "Amazon," even though, in mythology, the Amazons were a nation of warrior women who burned off their right breasts so they could use a bow and arrow more effectively in war.

We do not refrain from using the word "martial," meaning military, as in a statement like: "The town was under *martial* law," even though the word comes from *Mars,* the Roman god of war.

As we look into the night sky, we do not refrain from using the term "Milky Way," even though it comes from the myth that Juno, while nursing Mercury or Hercules, scattered milk across the sky.

We do not refrain from using names for planets such as Mercury, Venus, or Mars, even though these were originally pagan names. The book of Job even represents the Lord as saying: "Canst thou bind the sweet influences of *Pleiades,* or loose the bands of *Orion?* Canst thou bring forth *Mazaroth* in his season? or canst thou guide *Arcturus* with his sons?" (Job 38:31,32; cf. 9:9).

The *Pleiades*, in mythology, were the seven daughters of Atlas who were transformed by Jupiter into a group of stars when they were pursued by Orion. *Orion* was a giant hunter slain by Artemis, figured in the stars by a man with a sword, three stars on a line forming his belt. *Arcturus* is a fixed star near the tail of the Great Bear. *Mazaroth* is linked with the signs of the Zodiac.

The following words, gleaned from *The City of God* by Augustine (354-430 A.D.), show numerous links between the names of pagan deities and common words:

"...the goddess Stimula, who should *stimulate* to unusual action...the goddess Strenua, who should make them *strenuous*...to her whom they name Quies because she makes men *quiet*....But what does a man wish that he think Fortune also a goddess and worships her? [as giver of *fortune*]....why is Faith believed to be a goddess, and why does she herself receive temple and altar?....king Hostilius...introduced the new gods Fear and Dread...so of Virtus, who gives *virtue;* Honor, who gives *honor;* Concordia, who gives *concord;* Victoria, who gives *victory*..."[4]

Are words such as stimulate, strenuous, quiet, fortune, faith, fear, dread, virtue, honor, concord, and victory bad words simply because they were also the names of gods or goddesses? Should we refrain from using a Bible *Concordance* because there was a goddess named Concordia?

Language is made up of many elements. To try to do away with every word that once had some pagan linkage, would be fruitless. The Bible says: "Strive not about words to no profit" (2 Tim. 2:14). There would be no profit in wasting time trying to reinvent the English language.

While it is commendable that people do not want anything "pagan," unless this concept is kept in balance, it could lead to some strange extremes. One would not have a *Mercury* automobile or ride on the train *The California Zephyr*, since Mercury and Zephyr are names of pagan deities! And some would not own a Ford *Thunderbird!*

Among Indians, a mythological bird that caused thunder was called, simply enough, a "Thunderbird." I know some people who attended a meeting in which "preaching against paganism" included the condemnation of the T-bird automobile! Not wanting to own a "pagan" car or be under some Satanic curse, they quickly sold their car. This kind of reasoning can easily become mere superstition.

Pagan deities, along with the sun and the moon, have provided the basis for the naming of the days of the week: Sunday (Sun day), Monday (Moon day), Tuesday (Tiw's day), Wednesday (Woden's day), Thursday (Thor's day), Friday (Frig's day), and Saturday (Saturn's day). But these names are in such common use now, they no longer convey any pagan significance.

If we announce the church is going to have a "Friday night service," for example, no one would take this to mean we would be worshipping the goddess Frig. If we speak about a "Saturday service," no one would take this to mean we would be worshipping Saturn. A "Wednesday night prayer meeting," would not imply prayer would be offered to Woden!

How, then, is "Easter" any different? Even if the word came from an ancient goddess, it does not have that meaning now.

6. It is evident that a word can vary in meaning from one language to another.

What is a word anyhow? Merely letters that are no better, or worse, than the way they are perceived at any given time or place. If we are sending a present to someone in Germany, we should not write "gift" on the package, for gift in German means "poison"! In some countries cigarettes are called "fags." But imagine someone going into a convenience store in San Francisco and asking for a pack of fags!

The term "White House" causes us to immediately think of the presidential mansion in Washington D.C. Yet if we hear the term "Casa Blanca," though it is the spanish equivalent, most think of a city in Morocco or the classic Humphrey Bogart movie!

If we say "Red Pole," how many would think of Baton Rouge, the capital of Louisiana? Yet this is exactly what the French words mean!

"Santa Ana" is the name of a city in southern California, which is but the Spanish form of St. Anne, the legendary name of Mary's mother. But by bringing the Spanish form over into English, Santa

Ana acquires its own distinct meaning. If a church located there chose the name "Community Church of Santa Ana," this would be understood as a church in the *city* of Santa Ana. This would not mean people who gathered there worshipped St. Anne.

If at another time and place a word similar to Easter was in use—as the name of a goddess—when it found its place in the English language it did not retain that meaning. It is doubtful if the word in English ever designated a day to worship a pagan goddess.

"EASTER" IN KING JAMES VERSION

The word "Easter" appears one time in the King James Version of the Bible, in Acts 12:4: "...intending after *Easter* to bring him forth to the people." It is acknowledged on all sides that the Greek word here is *Pascha*, meaning "Passover," and for which the word Easter is not a literal translation. Are we to assume, then, that the King James translator of this passage was trying to promote "paganism"? Not at all! There is an explanation.

For centuries the Bible was locked up in the Latin language which was meaningless to the majority of people. As the Bible began to be translated into the languages common people could understand, there was a distinct emphasis on trying to make the meaning clear. In the process, translators faced a dilemma: Should they always try to make an *exact* translation, even though a word they used might not be as clear to readers? Or, should they use a word that would better convey the overall meaning, though not an exact translation?

By the time the Bible was translated into English, the word Easter was clearly linked with the season we call spring. It did not convey an idolatrous meaning, for English Bibles, such as Tyndale's and Coverdale's, "frequently used Easter as the translation of *Pascha* (Passover)"[5]—even in Matthew 26:2,19, etc. These translators evidently felt that English readers, being non-Jewish, would easier understand what season was intended by using the word Easter, instead of Passover. Since Easter and Passover both occur in spring, it was not a totally invalid word choice.

Were men like Coverdale and Tyndale insincere? Were they Satan's agents, out to promote paganism by inserting the word "Easter" into the Bible? Were they part of a conspiracy to deceive people into worshipping a pagan goddess? Absolutely not! William Tyndale, far from being a compromiser, suffered persecution and, ultimately, martyrdom in 1536 for his efforts to promote the Bible!

In 1611, about 90 percent of Tyndale's translation became the basis of the King James version.[6] Only in one place, however, was the word Easter retained (Acts 12:4). Most Bible readers today understand that "Passover"—and consequently the time of Jesus' death and resurrection—occurred in the spring of the year. None of the newer English translations use the term Easter. All, including the *New King James Version,* use the term Passover.

It should be kept in mind that Christians celebrated the resurrection of Christ long before someone in the eighth century attached the word Easter to it. The addition of this word did not suddenly change the celebration into a pagan observance!

What is called Easter in English-speaking countries, is called "The Great Day" among Eastern Slavs. They greet one another, as do the Greeks, with the words, "Christ is risen!" receiving the response, "He is risen indeed!"

The same celebration in Spain is called *Pasha,* in Russia *Pashka,* in France *Paque,* in Italy *Pasqua,* etc.—words that mean "Passover." Does this make the celebration in these countries "Jewish"? No one believes that. It follows then, if English speaking Christians use the word Easter for the same celebration, the word itself cannot make it "pagan."

CONSTANTINE AND THE COUNCIL

We have heard it said that "Easter is nothing but a Roman Catholic holiday"—that "Constantine started Easter"—that "it all came out of the Nicene Council"! This is misinformation. Anyone who has looked into the evidence knows better.

Christ's resurrection was being celebrated by Christians long before anything resembling what is known today as the Roman Catholic church developed, and has been widely celebrated by churches that are not, and never were, under the headship of Rome.

The location of Nicaea was far from Rome, located in what is now called Turkey—in the area of the Eastern Church, from which the bulk of the ministers in attendance came. The bishop of Rome (the Pope) did not even attend the council, but was represented by a delegate, Hosius of Cordova.

Constantine, who played a prominent part in the Nicene Council, was a man with glaring inconsistencies in his life. Even so, this does not mean that God could not have used him to accomplish certain things. We recall that God anointed king Cyrus, even though he did not know the Lord, to bring about blessings for the people of God in the Old Testament (Isa. 45:1-13; Ezr. 1:1-3).

Constantine did some good things: He did away with death by crucifixion, opposed the worship of Tammuz, and made provision for churches to be built. He sought to end the persecution of Christians that had been so brutal.

At the Nicene Council, it is said that he kissed the wounds of those who had been tortured and maimed for the cause of Christ—men like Paulus, a minister of Neo-Caesarea on the Euphrates, who had been deprived of the use of both hands by the application of a red-hot iron by the order of Licinius. Both Potamon and Spiridion of Cyprus had lost their right eyes; others at the Council had lost their right arms. Paphnutius of Upper Thebes, had lost his right eye and both his legs in the Maximinian persecution. Some who attended the Council were later martyred, such as Hypatius. To accuse such men of being insincere impostors, can hardly be justified.

In different countries, different ways of figuring the time for Easter had developed. Neither Constantine nor those who attended the Nicene Council *started* Easter; they simply sought to establish a uniform time for the spring celebration.

There were those who favored using a set date of a month, rather than a fixed day of the week. The Syrian Christians held their celebration on the first day of the week—the Sunday after the Jews kept the Passover. At Antioch, this was also the practice. In Rome and Alexandria, Easter was celebrated on the Sunday that followed the first full moon after the spring equinox. But in Rome, the equinox fell on March 25, while in Alexandria, located further south, it was March 21. In Gaul, a number of ministers used a fixed date, figuring Christ's death on March 25 and his resurrection on March 27. The Montanists in Asia Minor kept Easter on the Sunday after April 6.

For the Nicene Council to establish a time on which everyone would agree, was no easy task. Should they use a fixed day of the year, or a fixed day of the week? It could not be both. Since the resurrection of Christ had been on the first day of the week—Sunday—many favored the celebration on this day. (All Christians in the early centuries, as far as we know, agreed this was the day Christ arose from the dead; none believed he rose late on Saturday afternoon or on some other day—see my book *"Three Days and Three Nights"—Reconsidered in the Light of Scripture*).

As to which Sunday in spring would be set aside to commemorate the resurrection, a plan was worked out whereby it would be the first Sunday after the full moon that follows the spring equinox. As a result, right or wrong, Easter is observed each year between March 22 and April 25 by our calendar.

Because the annual observance of Christ's resurrection grew out of the Jewish Passover, some feel it would be better to use a fixed date (regardless of the day of the week), taking the Lord's supper at Passover time on the same night he did. On several occasions, I have had the opportunity to speak at such services and partake of the Lord's supper. But dogmatism about an *exact* date for this cannot be justified any more than an *exact* date for Easter. As *The Encyclopedia Britannica* phrases it, the subject is a "very difficult and complex one."

A pastor friend of mine—though his church takes the Lord's supper each year at Passover time—after spending years studying the matter, came to this conclusion: There is absolutely no way to determine which night on our calendar would correspond with the exact night on which Jesus instituted the Lord's supper. Does this seem surprising? Even among the Jewish people, as we shall see, the Passover itself was not always on a totally uniform date at the time of Christ!

In the Bible, months were figured by the moon (lunar time), each new moon starting a new month (1 Sam. 20:18-34, etc.). The Hebrew word translated "new moon" is the same word translated "month" (Strong's Concordance, 2320). But 12 months, figured by the moon, amount to only 354 days—11 days short of being a year, as figured by the sun (solar time). For this reason, it was necessary to add a month *about* every three years, otherwise the feast days that were linked with ripened harvests, would not come at the right time of year.

The first spring month began the grain harvest; consequently if the crop was not far enough along so that the wave sheaf could be offered, an extra month (called Veadar) would be added. In this case, Passover would occur a month later than it would when the extra month was not added![7]

The Jewish calendar in use today adds the extra month on a calculated and fixed basis—in a 19-year cycle, it is added in the 3rd, 6th, 8th, 11th, 14th, 17th, and 19th years. This keeps lunar reckoning in step with solar reckoning. But at the time of Christ, the extra month was *arbitrarily* added, with even the rules about how and when to do this varying from time to time. Because we have no way to know in which years a month was added, to make claims about an exact corresponding date on *our* calendar for the Last Supper is out of the question.

The day on which a month began—from which the 14 days to Passover were counted—could vary also. Observation of the new moon began the month, but the contour of the land, a hill being in the way, or cloudy weather could interfere. If the arc of vision above the horizon was between 9 and 14 degrees, the new moon was not visible in all of Palestine on the same day. And what about Jews living in other countries? Jewish leaders struggled with these problems for centuries.

As time went on, they decided the Mount of Olives should be used as the proper place for observation and a system of reporting and relaying the appearance of the new moon was worked out. Ultimately, calculation was substituted for observation, but this type of calendar came much later, such being introduced by Hillel II about A.D. 360.

Because of the uncertainty about the new moon, Jews living in Babylonian and Alexandrian communities were advised "to follow the custom of their fathers and continue to celebrate two days, advice which was followed, and is still followed, by the majority of Jews living outside of Palestine."[8]

In Matthew, Mark, and Luke, the time of the Last Supper was on the Passover (Lk. 22:13-15); but in John, Passover is mentioned as being the following day (John 18:28). Some believe there had been a difficulty confirming the new moon that month, or some other problem, so that the Calendar Court had sanctioned two days, each of which could be called Passover, that year.

Because there is no way to know in which years an extra month was added, or how consistent some of the new moon observations were in the first century, there is no way now to determine the exact date of the Last Supper. Nor will writing to the Naval Observatory in Washington, D.C. to ask for astronomical information, supply the answer. But does it really matter?

Some have wasted precious years studying calendars, complicated calculations, and fine points of the law that can really add nothing to that "so great a salvation" that is provided for us in Christ!

Some years ago, when I arrived at a man's house who had asked me to come see him, something on the front of his house caught my eye. It was a large clock encircled by a neon light and beneath which, also in neon, were the words: BIBLE TIME. My watch was obviously not on "Bible time"! This man, I learned, believed time should be kept, even in the United States, by *Jerusalem* time.

There are some Ultra-Orthodox Jews in Israel, according to the *Encyclopedia Judaica,* that are stricter than this: they do not even believe in clocks! Because there are 12 hours in a day (cf. John 11:9), they believe that from sunrise to sunset must always be figured as 12 hours, even though winter days are shorter, and summer days are longer. By this reckoning, an "hour" would need to vary from 49 to 71 minutes, depending on the season. No clock can do this!

Without questioning the sincerity of anyone, let me simply say this: I have yet to see any real spiritual fruitfulness come from extreme, overly strict, letter-of-the-law type doctrines. People who become too concerned about technical points, bog down with the details, failing to move ahead in the flow of the Holy Spirit.

FORTY DAYS OF LENT

It is not uncommon for those of the anti-Easter persuasion to make statements like: "Lent came right out of Babylon!"

Proof for this is sought in Hislop's *Two Babylons*: "The forty days' abstinence of Lent was directly borrowed from the worshippers of the Babylonian goddess."[9] But where is the proof? Hislop uses several disjointed examples, such as a 40 day observance of some Devil worshippers in Koordistan. He cites Layard's *Nineveh and Babylon*, for this. But if one takes the time to find this old book, as I have done, he will fail to find any connection with ancient Babylon or a goddess of any kind.

The Devil worshippers, the Yezidis, visited by Layard 150 years ago, were an illiterate people, believing it was wrong to read or write. They were sometimes called Devil worshippers because they feared the Devil. In their strange belief system, they also believed in Christ, that he "will come to govern the world, but that after him Sheikh Medi will appear, to whom will be given special jurisdiction." Their religious practices included things they adopted from Jews, Christians, and Muslims. So when we read: "There are forty days fast in the spring of the year, but they are observed by few; one person in a family may fast for the rest,"[10] it is more likely they had obtained this concept from a Christian custom, not from ancient Babylon—from which they would have been separated by thousands of years!

Might we suggest that the 40 days of Lent that developed among Christians did not come from *Babylon,* but from the *Bible?*

In the Bible the number *forty* is often linked with humiliation, affliction, and punishment:

Moses twice humbled himself in fasting and prayer *forty* days and *forty* nights (Deut. 9:9,18).

Elijah fasted *forty* days (1 Kings 19:8).

Jesus fasted *forty* days (Matt. 4:2).

Forty years Israel was afflicted in the wilderness (Num. 14:33,34).

Forty years Egypt was desolate for treacherous dealing with Israel (Eze. 29:11-13).

Forty days a new mother was in purification following the birth of a male child, and twice *forty* days for a female child (Lev. 12:4,5).

Forty days and *forty* nights it rained at the time of Noah's flood (Gen. 7:12).

Forty days did Ezekiel bear the iniquity of the house of Judah (Eze. 4:6).

Jonah preached that Nineveh would be overthrown in *forty* days (Jonah 3:4).

It was *forty* days after his resurrection that Christ ascended into heaven (Acts 1:3,9).

Forty stripes were allowed under Mosaic law as punishment (Deut. 25:3).

Without arguing that such references provide any Biblical command for Lent, I think any unbiased person would agree: Considering the evidence, it is far more likely that the significance of the number forty came from the Bible, not from Babylon.

Setting aside a time for fasting in the early church was based—not on paganism—but on the words of Jesus: "...the days will come, when the bridegroom shall be taken from them, *and then shall they fast*" (Matt. 9:15). According to Irenaeus, some fasted one day, others two, some for the length of time between Christ's death and resurrection, and some longer. Fasting practices also varied in rigor.

In Alexandria, around 250 A.D., some fasted during the whole week before resurrection day. By the time of the Nicene Council (A.D. 325), a period of 40 days for Lent had become "a well-established custom"[11]—*it did not start then!*

In my own Christian experience, I have never observed Lent, as such. Fasting for me—whether complete fasting or partial fasting—has been linked more with situations, not seasons.

But I am not going to condemn all these early Christians who may have developed a custom I find unnecessary. They were not infallible any more than we are. Most of them did not know how to read or write, were not able to study the Bible, nor did they have a Bible to study! In simple faith, they believed

Jesus died and rose again. Their lives were changed through faith in Him. For some of them it was meaningful to set aside special times of fasting at the season of Christ's death and resurrection. If some chose to begin their period of fasting by using ashes as a sign of sorrow or repentance, the use of ashes was not without Biblical precedent (2 Sam. 13:19; Esth. 4:1,3; Job 42:6; Jer. 6:26; Dan. 9:3; Matt. 11:21).

But the problem, as I see it, is that some practices that may have once been spiritually meaningful, over a period of time can degenerate into mere forms and ceremonies. People continue to follow the form of godliness, but without the power thereof. It becomes religion without reality. What may have stemmed from heartfelt conviction, becomes institutionalized.

I once heard an evangelist preach on "Keys of the Kingdom." At the end of the message, he dumped out a container with many keys around the area in front of the platform. All were invited to come forward and pick up keys, in faith, for whatever needs they had—spiritually, physically, or financially. Because of this unique illustration, I still remember that message.

The use of objects to illustrate a sermon is within the guidelines of scripture (Jer. 13:1-11; 18:1-6; Matt. 18:2; Acts 21:11, etc.). But, let's suppose that this became a ritual. Every month we preached on "Keys of the Kingdom" and threw out keys for people to pick up! What was effective at one time, could easily become ineffective and a mere form later on.

For many, this is what has happened to Ash Wednesday and Lent. These things may not be bad in themselves, but they have become mere forms, religious habits, void of any real power of the Holy Spirit. The glaring inconsistency of Mardi Gras, or Carnival, as it is called in some countries, provides a vivid example.

Most are familiar with the food product known as *pretzels*. According to one writer, "Pretzels were once a special *Lenten food,* particularly in Austria, Germany, and Poland. The word *Brezel* probably comes from *brachiatus,* having branchlike arms. The shape of the pretzel reminded someone of arms folded in prayer. They were first made in the fifth century *at the Vatican* and later were distributed to poor people on certain days of Lent....Only in the last century have they been available all year round."[12]

If pretzels were first made at the Vatican, it could be said that "pretzels came out of Roman Catholicism." By the reasoning of some, this would be a basis for preaching against eating pretzels! What might the sermon title be? *"Pagan Pretzels!"* The fact is, of course, pretzels are in such general use, the place of their origin or any original association with Lent, is no longer significant.

EASTER EGGS

What seems especially offensive to some about Easter is the seasonal trim: things like colored eggs and bunnies. And so, we must ask: Are people who color eggs and hide them for their children, committing idolatry? Are they performing a "fertility" rite?

In an effort to condemn Easter eggs, anti-Easter literature commonly presents numerous examples in which pagan people used eggs in rituals or ceremonies:

The ancient Druids bore an egg as a sacred emblem. In the rites of Bacchus at Athens, an egg was consecrated during a nighttime ceremony. A Hindu fable mentions a golden colored egg. A sect in Japan regarded a brazen egg as sacred. Painted eggs have been used in religious festivals in China. Eggs were hung up in temples in Greece and Egypt, etc.

I don't think there is any doubt that pagans used eggs in various ways, but the weakness of presenting such examples is that they are unrelated to each other, disjointed, obscure, and with no real connection to Easter eggs as we know them today. Only by emphasizing one similarity—the use of eggs—and ignoring a whole multitude of differences, can this argument have any force at all.

To read anti-Easter literature, one could easily conclude that the egg symbolizes something sinful, wicked, abominable, pagan! This is misleading, for among the many ancient people who were intrigued with the egg, most regarded it as a symbol of *new life*. This is not bad symbolism.

An egg, though appearing as a lifeless object in one moment, can in another moment burst forth with new life! Not having the revelation of the true Creator, some primitive people carried it further, even supposing that the earth itself must have hatched from an egg. Of course no one believes that now!

Among Hindu legends, the figure of Brahma sat inside a golden egg, floating in the primeval waters for a thousand years, with land, sea, mountains, planets, gods, and mankind all inside the egg with him. In Chinese legend, P'an Ku, the first man, emerged from a cosmic egg, as did Sun Wu-k'ung, the popular monkey king of Taoist and Buddhist legend. In another myth, an egg of wondrous size fell from heaven into the Euphrates river, fish rolled it to the bank, doves settled on it, and from which the goddess Venus was hatched.

Because eggs were commonly recognized as a symbol of new life, it was only a natural development that such would ultimately come to be associated with spring, the time of year when all nature blossoms forth with new life. That today's custom of using Easter eggs probably grew out of such earlier beliefs, is no secret. Even *The Catholic Encyclopedia* says: "The custom may have its origin in paganism."[13]

There was a time when some of us reasoned that if anything was once pagan, it must still be pagan! This is not necessarily true. Consider, for example, the following quotation from *Hastings' Dictionary of the Bible*:

"Athletic contests...originated in pre-historic times, and were closely associated with *religious worship*. Thus the Olympic games were held in honor of Olympian Zeus in connection with the magnificent temple in Olympia in Elis; the Isthmian games on the Isthmus of Corinth in honor of Poseidon; the Pythian were associated with the worship of the Pythian Apollo at Delphi; the Nemean were celebrated at Nemea, a valley of Argolis, to commemorate the Nemean Zeus."[14]

Today, athletic contests are secular—no one supposes they honor gods like Zeus, Poseidon or Apollo! Because the pagan linkage no longer exits, there is no valid reason to condemn sports as being pagan. Imagine parents not allowing their child to sign up for the Little League baseball team—since sports contests "came from paganism"!

Why is it, that some can accept this distinction regarding sports, and a host of other things, but insist that a seasonal child's game, an innocent coloring and hiding of eggs, is still pagan?

While conducting evangelistic meetings in Delaware some years ago, a pastor's wife shared with me a memory from her childhood. As a child, she had never eaten popcorn. She had only smelled the aroma of hot buttered popcorn as she walked by the entrance of the downtown movie theater—an aroma that seemed so good! Having been taught that the movie theater was evil, *she assumed that eating popcorn was evil also!* She later realized, of course, there was no valid linkage between the two things. But even as an adult, when eating popcorn, she would recall that childhood belief.

In somewhat the same way, there are those who tend to make big issues out of non-issues; to make things into idolatry that are not idolatrous; to equate things with paganism when there is really no connection.

"But what do things like bunnies and eggs have to do with Christ's resurrection?" some ask. This is easy to answer. *Nothing.* And, this is the point! I am not aware of *anyone* who supposes they do! Eggs, bunnies, and the like, are separate—mere decorations, cultural accessaries, generally recognized symbols of the spring season—no more than that.

Those who are of the anti-Easter persuasion, commonly fail to acknowledge this distinction. If the movie is bad, the popcorn is bad! They merge it all together, to make it appear that those who celebrate Easter place all of these things on the same level.

If this were the case—if people believed that "eggs" or "rabbits" had anything to do with salvation, if they were bowing down to them, if such were anything more than seasonal decorations—I would be the first to condemn such practices as superstitious and wrong.

Churches sometimes use the symbol of a dove, representing the Holy Spirit, above the baptistry or on the wall above the platform. It is not an inappropriate symbol, in that the Holy Spirit, like a dove, did indeed descend upon Jesus at his baptism (John 1:32). But they would never think of using the symbol of a rabbit in this way! Clearly this shows a distinction is made.

When I was a boy, we dyed Easter eggs and hid them. Over the years since then—in different circumstances, and on different occasions—I have been with families who hid Easter eggs for children and grandchildren to find. Not once did any of them do this as a religious ceremony. Not once did any of them claim it was a command from God. And, certainly none of them did it as a pagan "fertility rite"!

It could be argued that coloring eggs and hiding them is a waste of time and money. It could be argued that it is inconsistent (in that many children who hunt for eggs do not like to eat them!). It could be argued, quite correctly, there is no Biblical command for the practice. But to say that Christian people who hide Easter eggs for their children are practicing a pagan fertility rite—*no!* This is not true. Is there even *one* person, *anywhere,* who does this as a fertility rite?

In primitive times, of course, fertility rites were widely practiced. As strange as it sounds today, even an early form of football was a fertility rite!

According to *Browser's Book of Beginnings*, "The earliest evidence of a game that featured two opposing teams kicking, tossing, and aggressively advancing a ball in opposite directions is found in an ancient Egyptian fertility rite"—5,000 years ago.[15]

So would any insist that football is a fertility rite? Imagine a parent sending a note to the school: "My son is not to play football with his class—it's pagan"!

If someone wanted to find fault with football, he could talk about brutality, about the obsession it becomes with some, that there are better things to do, and similar arguments. But to argue that football is wrong because it is a pagan "fertility rite"? The very thought is so ridiculous, it is laughable. Yet, to some extent, it is by this same type of reasoning that some would condemn Easter eggs. They refuse to allow the obvious: Some ancient and obscure "origin" does not necessarily dictate a present meaning.

Visitors arriving in Hawaii, for example, are commonly greeted with the word *Aloha* and garlanded with leis, a lei being a wreath or necklace of flower blossoms. It is a friendly, warm, traditional Hawaiian greeting. If at one time this practice conveyed some other meaning—linked with fertility and sexual superstition—it does not have that meaning now!

But if one wanted to "strain at a gnat and swallow a camel," he could argue that the use of flower garlands is pagan; that garlands, being round, are idolatrous; and that even the Bible shows they were used by the priests of Jupiter! (Acts 14:13).

To suppose that something is idolatrous because it is *round*—like the sun—fails to take into account that the wayward son who returned to Father's House had a *round* ring placed on his finger, and a *round* crown is symbolic of a Christian's reward (Lk. 15:22; 2 Tim. 4:8). Why are rings and crowns round—because they are pagan? No; they are round because God made fingers and heads round. If rings and crowns were square, they would not fit!

People who are welcomed to Hawaii by having leis placed around their necks are not honoring some pagan god or performing a fertility ritual; nor are people who use Easter eggs.

Granted there were ancient tribes that performed abominable fertility rites, but this does not mean that fertility itself is wrong. Historically, the fertility of crops and people often meant the very survival of the tribe. It was a form of "blessing" to wish fertility for someone, as when it was said to Rebekah, "Be thou the mother of *thousands of millions*"! (Gen. 24:60). A *lack* of fertility was considered a "reproach" (Lk. 1:25).

In the Bible, the word "fruitful," meaning fertility, appears 35 times. Promises about being "exceeding *fruitful*" (Gen. 17:6), having a *"fruitful* field" (Isa. 32:15), or being *"fruitful"* in good works (Col. 1:10), were used in a *good* sense.

While the Bible does not expressly use the egg as a symbol of fertility—eggs only being mentioned nine times and in a general way—fertility symbols are certainly not absent from its pages!

In Eastern countries, the many-seeded pomegranate was regarded as a fertility symbol. Pomegranates alternated with bells on the robe of the high priest (Exod. 39:24). Four hundred pomegranates adorned the two pillars in front of the Jerusalem temple (2 Chron. 4:13). The Israelites did not refrain from using pomegranates as decorations, even though pagans in nearby Syria worshipped a god named Rimmon, meaning "Pomegranate"! (2 Kings 5:18; Strong's Concordance, 7417, 7416). Temple decorations also included carvings of palm trees, open flowers, and *lilies* (1 Kings 6:29; 7:22, 26).

Even something as common as water was regarded as a symbol of life, God's blessings being likened to rain, showers, fountains, wells, and rivers (Ps. 36:8; Isa. 33:21; Joel 2:23; Ezek. 34:26). At the time of Jesus, during a ceremony the Jewish people had developed, a priest drew water from the pool of Siloam in a golden vessel. With pomp and ceremony —and with people singing the words, "With joy shall ye draw water out of the wells of salvation" (Isa. 12:6)—the water was brought into the temple and poured out on the altar. It was on this occasion, when people were thinking about the symbolism of water, that Jesus cried out: "If any man thirst, let him come unto me and drink" (John 7:37).

This ceremony was not spelled out in scripture —there was no "command" to do this at the feast—still, the symbolism of water was valid and Jesus did not condemn it. Instead, he simply used the occasion as an opportunity to point people to the true water of salvation that is found in Him!

Even the *springing* forth of nature—from which we logically get our word "spring" (the season)—provides a positive metaphor in the scriptures: "As the garden causes the things that are sown in it to *spring* forth; so the Lord God will cause righteousness and praise to *spring* forth before all the nations" (Isa. 61:11). "And they shall *spring* up as among the grass, as willows by the water courses" (Isa. 44:4). "Truth shall *spring* out of the earth" (Ps. 85:11). "The pastures of the wilderness do *spring*" (Joel 2:22), etc.

That the spring season can be a symbol of new life is acknowledged on all sides. This is in beautiful harmony with the fact that Christ rose again from the dead in the spring of the year, providing "new life" for those who trust in Him!

Eggs, also being widely recognized as a symbol of new life, need not be regarded as evil. Even rabbits, known for their fertility, need not be looked on as evil. Swine, serpents, scorpions, or spiders might better serve as evil symbols (Matt. 7:6; Lk. 10:19); but eggs and rabbits are not in this category.

A fine Christian man phoned me prior to Easter one year, quite concerned about a situation he faced where he worked. Part of his job was to unload trucks with a wide variety of merchandise, including some crates with stuffed, artificial rabbits for Easter. Since he did not believe in Easter rabbits, he questioned whether he should quit his job. He had a wife and children to support. My advice to him was to keep his job. *He was not committing idolatry by unloading rabbits!*

The members of one little family may decorate some Easter eggs and hide them in the yard. Though pursuing a seasonal custom, in no way are they committing idolatry! They love the Lord. Their lives have been changed by Him. They are upbeat believers, with a good spirit. But nearby is a neighbor that is bitter against Easter. People who celebrate Easter, he argues, are really worshipping Baal! He is judgmental. He "knows" that eggs are pagan! Suppose they are—they could not be any worse than a bad attitude.

This is not to say that everyone who advocates the anti-Easter position has a bad attitude. But the potential is there. Christians who celebrate Easter can accept, as Christians, those who do not; but it is more difficult for this to work the other way. How can people who "worship Baal" be Christians!

During the years when I echoed some of the anti-Easter concepts in my writings—unaware there was another side to the coin—I received very little, *if any,* criticism for this position. In fact, it was very *popular!* The criticism has come from the other side. I have received mean-spirited letters accusing me of being a modern-day Demas who has forsaken the Lord, that I have compromised with the "Great Whore," that by failing to warn people against the evils of Christmas and Easter I will send souls to Hell, that the same type of demons that empowered Joseph Goebbels (Hitler's propaganda aide) have caused me to modify my position!

Please be assured, it is not my purpose to glorify rabbits or eggs, but only to encourage a sensible balance. If some feel that things such as Easter eggs are not pleasing to the Lord, my advice is simple: Follow your conscience and conviction. But there is no need to cause division, accusing other Christians of being Baal worshippers! Within the guidelines of Romans 14, we should be willing to accept one another, not reject one another over non-essential points.

EASTER SUNRISE SERVICES

I have before me, as I write, a booklet which says this about Easter sunrise services: "Deceived into believing this is Christian...millions practice every Easter the identical form of the ancient sun worship of the sun god Baal!...the most abominable of all idolatry." *What?* Christians worshipping Baal at sunrise services?

Justification for such wild statements is commonly sought in Ezekiel's words about "five and twenty men, with...their faces toward the *east;* and they worshipped the *sun toward the east,*" such things being called "abominations" (Ezek. 8:14-17).

Since the sun is in the east at sunrise, the time Ezekiel described was indeed sunrise or early morning. There is this *similarity.* But the *differences* are drastic! Ezekiel described men who worshipped the *sun.* Christians do not worship the sun; they worship Christ. Christians who attend an Easter sunrise service will hear a message about an *empty* tomb and a resurrected Savior who lives *today!*

Having such a service *at sunrise* does not come from paganism, but from the *Bible.* It was at sunrise that the women came to the tomb and discovered it was empty: "And very early in the morning the first day of the week, they came unto the sepulchre

AT THE RISING OF THE SUN" (Mk. 16:2). If some choose to argue against this, they must argue against the Bible itself.

WEEPING FOR TAMMUZ

When Ezekiel spoke of men worshipping the sun toward the east, he also saw "women weeping for Tammuz" (Ezek. 8:14-16). Those who say this is the origin of today's Easter observance really miss the mark. The time of "weeping for Tammuz" was not in spring (Easter), but in *summer!*

As the *Theological Wordbook of the Old Testament* points out, this ritual drama "was based on the observable fact that the end of spring brought the end of new life in nature...the obvious conclusion was that Tammuz, the power who had produced all these blessings, had died! So a dramatic lament for the dead god was held annually at the beginning of the *hot, dry summer,* in the fourth month of the Mesopotamian calendar (our late June and early July), the month that was named 'Tammuz' after him."[16] This month—in summer—is still called Tammuz in the Jewish calendar.

So the time of "weeping for Tammuz" was in summer, not spring. Again the anti-Easter literature is in error!

The World Book Encyclopedia says that "some scholars believe the word Easter comes from the early German word *eostarun*, which means *dawn.*"[17] This is not impossible. Because dawn occurs in the *east*, the very spelling of "East-er" tends to reinforce this position. But from this point, two conflicting opinions emerge:

Those of the anti-Easter persuasion would lump sun worship (Ezekiel 8:16), sunrise in the east, and East-er all together as a strong negative. One could be left with the impression that "east" is a bad word. But, others look on the dawn in the east as a symbol of a new day, of new beginning—a positive. And, in beautiful harmony with this, the very word that is translated "east" (dawn) in the New Testament is used as a metaphor of Jesus Christ!

Let me explain. The Greek word for east is *anatole*. It appears in Matthew 2:1, Luke 13:29, Revelation 21:13, etc. The word itself means "a rising of light, i.e. dawn" (Strong's Concordance, 395), and so provides a logical basis for the word east. It is this same exact word that is translated "Dayspring" or as the margin says, "Dawn"—referring to Jesus Christ (Luke 1:78).

If it is correct that the word Easter contains the meaning of *dawn*—dawn being in the east—then, according to the Bible, it would not be incorrect to refer to Christ as our "Easter"!

In another metaphor, Christ is called "the bright morning star" (Rev. 22:16), the morning star having linkage with the approach of *dawn.* The word "star" in the New Testament is *aster* (Strong's Concordance, 792). We cannot base conclusions on a similarity of letters, of course, but if we add an E to *aster,* we would have Easter.

Where the King James text refers to Christ as the "Dayspring" or "Dawn," *The New International Version* refers to him as: "...the rising sun...to shine on those living in darkness." As such, Christ was the fulfillment of Old Testament prophecy. Malachi had spoken of him as "the Sun of Righteousness," rising with healing in his wings (Mal. 4:2). It should be noticed that the term here is "S-U-N," not the more common "S-O-N."

The Biblical writers felt it entirely appropriate to use the rising sun in the east as a type of Christ who brings the light of truth to a darkened world! Despite the fact that there were ancient pagans who worshipped the sun, the Psalmist did not hesitate to say, "...the Lord God is a SUN" (Ps. 84:11). Such wording is not idolatrous, but very meaningful when understood spiritually.

Two Christian songs I recall, even now, from childhood days have a "sunshine" theme:

Heavenly sunshine, heavenly sunshine,
Flooding my soul with glory divine,
Heavenly sunshine, heavenly sunshine,
Hallelujah, Jesus is mine! [18]

There is sunshine in my soul today,
More glorious and bright;
Than glows in any earthly sky, for Jesus is my light!
Oh! there's sunshine, blessed sunshine;
While the peaceful happy moments roll,
When Jesus shows his smiling face,
There is sunshine in my soul. [19]

Were the writers of these songs trying to inject sun worship into the church? Were they trying to turn Christians into sun worshippers? Did they have a subtle agenda to turn Jesus into a pagan sun-god? It is absurd!

In the past, some of us were prone to ask questions like, "Where in the Bible did Peter or Paul ever conduct an Easter sunrise service?" This type of questioning does not prove anything. Do we ever read that Peter or Paul performed a wedding ceremony, conducted a funeral, or constructed a building for worship? Does the Bible ever say they organized a choir, published a hymn book, or founded a Bible college? Can we picture them wearing glasses or a necktie, appearing on television, driving a car, or riding in an airplane?

Are we, then, going to condemn all these things just because we never read in the Bible that Peter or Paul did them? This is not sound doctrine; such reasoning only leads to confusion. Having a desire to hold to the apostolic faith does not mean that the church cannot grow and develop (Eph. 2:20-22).

"Where does the Bible ever mention a minister performing a wedding ceremony?" a man asked me at a church where I spoke. Because there is no specific example of this in the Bible, he automatically assumed it was wrong! But because marriage is "honorable," was God's plan "from the beginning," and is such a serious and meaningful step in the life of a couple—why not involve a man of God in the ceremony?

While I encourage people to be "Bible Christians," there is no reason to assume that something is wrong simply because it is not mentioned in the Bible. It could be argued that the Bible never mentions closing one's eyes during prayer. Are we then going to waste time preaching *against* closing eyes during prayer as though this were some major doctrine?

If only things mentioned in the Bible are valid, we would have to question why the word "Bible" is not in the Bible!

I can tell you about a group that held such an extreme "Bible only" position, they would not sing hymns like "Amazing Grace" or "How Great Thou Art!" In their services they would only sing words *from the Bible*—mainly from the book of Psalms. They didn't want anything *added* to the Bible. But even with this strictness, they were still adding something: *the melody!* Since the Bible is made up of words, and does not include musical notes, there is no way to know what the original melodies were!

A very common argument some use against Easter is this: "The Bible tells us to remember Christ's *death* (1 Cor. 11:25,26)—it never tells us to remember his birth or resurrection!" So they are against *any* celebration to honor his birth. They may oppose birthday celebrations in general, will not allow their children to have or attend a birthday party, or have a birthday cake (especially a *round* one with *candles* on it!). And they oppose *any* celebration in honor of Christ's resurrection!

But this is trying to prove something by what the Bible does *not* say—an argument based on *silence*. The Bible does not say to celebrate Easter; but it does not say *not* to celebrate Easter, either. So this type of reasoning fails to make a point either way.

If one forms conclusions by what "the Bible does not say," he could even teach that God wanted a man's wife to work on the sabbath—even though everyone else was resting! The wording of the fourth commandment is this: "...thou shalt not do any work, *thou*, nor thy *son*, nor thy *daughter*, thy *manservant*, nor thy *maidservant*, nor thy *cattle*" (Exod. 20:9,10) —nothing is said about the wife. Did this mean she never got a day off?

There is no Biblical "command" for a church to have a New Year's Eve service. But does there need to be? At these services there will be singing, testimonies, and preaching. In contrast to worldly people who may celebrate by getting drunk and having parties, Christians who choose to attend a New Year's Eve service will be on their knees, praying the old year out and the new year in. On several occasions over the years I have spoken at such services. While they do not correspond in timing to the New Year of a Jewish calendar, opportunities to "preach the Word" are not inappropriate at any season (2 Tim. 4:2).

Suppose we lived in a Muslim country that had a holiday called "Koran Day"—a time they set aside to read the Koran. As Christians, suppose we decided to call it "Bible Day" instead, and encouraged people to read the Bible on this day. Suppose, then, in time "Bible Day" caught on, people were helped, blessed, or came to Christ through the reading of the Word. Would this be wrong? Would this suddenly turn us into Muslims? Or would this simply be a case of "overcoming evil with good"? (Rom. 12:21).

In our opinion, if substituting "Bible Day" for "Koran Day" proved to be spiritually fruitful, we could judge it by its fruits. It would not require some direct Biblical command.

In the Old Testament, in addition to the days that were *commanded* by God, some days were observed by *custom*. "It was a custom in Israel...the daughters of Israel went yearly to lament...four days in a year" (Jdg. 11:40). "The Jews of the villages ...made the fourteenth day of the month Adar a day of gladness and feasting, and a good day, and of sending portions one to another" (Est. 9:19). Jesus attended the Feast of Dedication which the Jews observed annually to celebrate the defeat of Antiochus (John 10:22,23). Other days, by custom, were set aside for fasting (Zech. 8:19).

Why, then, should we believe that *Christians* cannot also develop times of celebration in remembrance of Jesus Christ? If such times are fruitful and spiritually meaningful, the potential for great good is there.

If some similarity with an ancient spring festival makes Easter "totally pagan," the same could be said about the very days God commanded Israel to observe—not just the days they observed by custom. The New Moon, Trumpets, Passover, and the Feast of Tabernacles were all linked with the new moon or full moon. According to *Harper's Bible Dictionary*, this was a practice of the pagan Canaanites who observed the new moon and the full moon with festivities.[20]

Even *The Jewish Encyclopedia* says that the harvest festival of Pentecost was "probably a midsummer festival in origin and taken over from the Canaanites"; and in another place: "The third agricultural festival, like the other two, was taken over from the Canaanites."[21] It is not our purpose here to argue the point—we believe God gave Israel those feast days—but that there were similarities with earlier, pagan Canaanite feast days is apparent.

Sometimes people have branded a day as "pagan" when there is really no connection. By this method, even something as innocent as "Mother's Day" could be condemned! One could quote the following words from the *People's Almanac:* "The beginnings of this holiday may have been in the ancient spring festival known as Hilaria, dedicated to the mother goddess Cybele."[22]

It is true that in mythology, Cybele was a mother—the "Mother of the gods"—and she had a spring festival dedicated to her, but this is where the similarities end. Consider the differences! A scholarly work on mythology says: "Her priests, called Corybantes and Galli, were emasculated to commemorate the emasculation of Atys, the beloved of Cybele, and dressed like women to achieve unity with the goddess. Her festivals were celebrated with wild dances and orgiastic excesses amid the resounding music of drums and cymbals."[23]

This is not the origin of Mother's Day! Miss Anna Jarvis of Philadelphia, following her mother's death, promoted the idea of setting aside a day to honor all mothers. Eventually it gained support and was made official on May 9, 1914, by a proclamation of President Woodrow Wilson. If the day has been exploited by florists, greeting-card companies, and candy manufacturers, this still does not make it pagan!

There was a time when some of us formed conclusions based on mythology. If we found a parallel in mythology with some present-day custom or belief, we assumed it was automatically "pagan." Eventually I came to see that this was an unsound procedure, for by this method, one could take almost *any* imaginary story and do the same, even "Jack and the Beanstalk"!

In the story, Jack, a poor country boy, trades the family cow for a handful of magic beans, which grow into an enormous beanstalk that reaches high into the clouds. He climbs the beanstalk and finds himself in the castle of an unfriendly giant. Sensing Jack's presence, the giant cries out: "Fee, fie, fo, fum, I smell the blood of an Englishman!" But outwitting the giant, Jack is able to retrieve goods that had been stolen from his family, including an enchanted goose that lays golden eggs. He manages to escape and chops down the beanstalk, causing the giant to fall to his death. After this, Jack's family prospered.

Notice, now, how this story could be twisted around to make senseless conclusions:

> Those who were initiated into the mysteries will surely know the hidden meaning here. Since Nimrod was a "mighty one," a giant, who else could this giant be but Nimrod? And the tall beanstalk, soaring up into the clouds, what could this be but the tower of Babel? There the language was confused, explaining why abnormal words like fee, fie, fo, fum were spoken.
>
> The golden eggs, what could they be but Easter eggs, their golden color being in imitation of the sun!
>
> As to the identity of Jack, is it any coincidence that among rabbits—rabbits being in a special way associated with Easter—that many are called *Jack* rabbits? The giant sought to kill Jack; hunters hunt jack rabbits; and if any further confirmation is needed, one can read right in the Bible that Nimrod was a "mighty hunter"!
>
> Our word "lumberjack" must be derived from this incident of Jack cutting down the beanstalk. Even today, do not lumberjacks go into the forest and cut down Christmas trees? And don't people

place up high on the tree a star, the symbol of Nimrod?

Jack was rewarded; and so now we can understand why it is said that a gambler hits the "jackpot"!

In the Bible God promised to reward Jacob with many possessions. Was it not Jacob who saw a ladder reaching, like the beanstalk, high into the heavens? If we drop the letters *ob* from the name Jacob, and add *k,* we have "Jack." Is it not evident, then, that the story of Jack and the Beanstalk is but a later corruption, no doubt by the hand of a Chaldean, of the story of Jacob?

But in his mystery form, Jack had another identity. In the worship of the sun-god Baal, whether on birthday cakes or in religious rites, *candles* were used. Many have not realized how this ties in with Jack, for though the words sound innocent on the surface, it is clearly written in literature:

> Jack, be nimble; Jack, be quick;
> Jack, jump over the *candlestick.*

Such reasoning is so absurd and disjointed, after piecing it together, I hesitated to even use it lest someone take it seriously! But this is the way ancient and obscure myths have been used to form conclusions about pagan origins. It requires magnifying a few similarities, while minimizing or ignoring a multitude of differences.

Suppose that people in some ancient pagan group sang religious songs. So do Christians. Suppose they bowed on their knees and prayed. So do Christians. Suppose they had a collection of sacred writings. So do Christians. Suppose they used water in some initiation rite. So do Christians. Suppose they partook of a sacred meal. So do Christians. All would agree that these similarities would not make the pagan group *Christian!* How, then, can a few seemingly pagan similarities make a Christian group *pagan?*

In 1983, I was invited to go with a group of ministers (of various denominations) on a study tour to Israel, Jordan, and Egypt. While visiting the ruins of an ancient temple along the Nile River, we happened to meet and shake hands with former President Jimmy Carter who was also visiting Egypt at the time. He mentioned attending services at a Coptic church that morning. On tours of the Bible lands, a person might visit a variety of places: Muslim mosques, Jewish synagogues, historic Christian churches and various other religious shrines. Perhaps inspired by this variety, when I returned home, I decided to do a local "tour" by visiting churches I had never been to before.

On Easter, because of the variation of service times, I was able on the same morning to attend a Southern Baptist, Roman Catholic, Latter Day Saints (Mormon), and Community Church (Presbyterian). As varied as these denominations are, *every one of them preached a positive message regarding the resurrection of Christ!* None regarded him as still dead in the tomb, but *alive* and in heaven as the risen Lord!

Had scheduling made it possible, I could have attended an Assembly of God, Church of the Nazarene, Church of God, Evangelical Free, Methodist, Church of Christ, Foursquare, and numerous others—all who would have preached the message of the resurrection!

Now please understand, I am not placing all of these various denominations on the same level. I am not saying one is as good as another. But what I am saying is this: In whatever areas any of them need to be faulted, criticized, or corrected, it is not because they preach that Jesus Christ rose from the dead! On this they are *right!*

Even at the time of Paul, everyone who preached Christ did not do so from the best motives. "Some preach Christ even of envy and strife," he wrote, "and some of good will: the one preach Christ of contention, not sincerely...but the other of love....What then, notwithstanding, every way, whether in pretense, or in truth, CHRIST IS PREACHED; and I therein do rejoice, yea, and will *rejoice"* (Phil. 1:15-18).

The message of Christ's resurrection—"He is not here, for He has risen"—known at first by only a few, has now circled the world so that millions have heard the glad news. We rejoice in this! If, in the process, some things fall short of God's best, He will ultimately judge or justify, and sort it all out.

NEW LIFE IN CHRIST

According to the Bible, not *all* traditions are bad (2 Thess. 2:15). If Easter is merely a "traditional" celebration, is God able to use even this for his glory? Indeed!

Because it was the "traditional" thing to do, years ago a man who did not know the Lord, went to church on Easter. Fortunately, the church he chose to attend was a gospel-preaching church. He heard the glad news that Christ, who died for our sins, rose again from the dead and is alive forevermore! That very morning, in that service, he received Jesus Christ as his Lord and Savior.

His whole life was changed! Old things passed away and all things became new (2 Cor. 5:17). Eventually he enrolled in Bible College to prepare for the ministry. Later this man, G. Willard Stearns —who initially came to Christ on Easter—was my pastor when I was a teenager and under whom I had my own beginnings in the Lord's work!

We know that valid worship must be "in spirit and in *truth*" (John 4:24). Some say there is no truth in Easter, so it is false worship. But consider these things:

They claim that "Easter" is the name of a pagan goddess. The truth is, *if* this was ever the case, this could only be an *obsolete* meaning now.

They criticize Easter eggs as though they are used as objects of worship. The truth is, people who color and hide Easter eggs with their children *never* use them as objects of worship.

They say that the Easter sunrise service was adopted from pagan sun worship. The truth is, sunrise services are conducted at this time because the empty tomb of Christ was discovered "at the rising of the sun."

They say that the 40 days of Lent came from ancient Babylon. The truth is, there is *much more* evidence to suggest that the significance of 40 days came from the Bible!

They say it was Constantine who brought Easter into the professing church at the Nicene Council in 325 A.D. The truth is, Christians celebrated the resurrection of Christ long before the time of Constantine.

So, we must ask, Who is telling the *truth?*

Christians who gather to celebrate the resurrection of Christ, whether they call it Easter or some other name, are *not* worshipping a pagan goddess! Anyone who makes this claim does not even have the gender right: Christians worship "the MAN Christ Jesus" (1 Tim. 2:5)—not a FEMALE goddess. Even with the emphasis that many Roman Catholics place on Mary, they do not observe Easter as Mary's day!

Years ago, when President Calvin Coolidge had returned from church, he was asked what the minister spoke about that morning. Coolidge, said to be a man of few words, replied:

"Sin."

When he was pressed as to what the preacher said about sin, he responded:

"I think he was against it."

Sin is a serious issue, we must be against it. It is so serious that "Christ died for our sins" (1 Cor. 15:3). But if we make "sin" out of things that are not sinful, we miss the mark. Those who preach that dedicated and victorious Christians are committing *sin* because they celebrate the resurrection of Christ, only cause confusion and needless division.

The fact that practically every pagan religion had some religious festival at the spring season is no marvel, this being the time of year when nature springs forth with new life. We might cite a *thousand* examples; what would this prove? Christians do not celebrate the Resurrection in spring because pagans had spring festivals. They celebrate in spring because this is the time of year Christ rose from the dead!

Jesus Christ, the Lamb of God, became our Passover, dying for our sins. But death could not destroy him, the grave could not contain him. He rose again on the third day! And so we remember not only his death, but also his resurrection. For, "if Christ be not risen, then is our preaching vain, and your faith is also vain" (1 Cor. 15:14).

Because He lives we have hope! Because He lives it is the dawn of a new day! Because He lives, it is springtime in our souls! Because He lives, we can live also—forever!

"Christ is risen!"

"He is risen indeed!"

NOTES

1. *The Encyclopedia of Religions* (New York: Macmillan Publishing Co., 1987), article: "Easter."
2. Rachel Hartman, *The Joys of Easter* (New York: Meredith Press, 1967), p. 71.
3. *Family Word Finder—A New Thesaurus of Synonyms and Antonyms in Dictionary Form* (Pleasantville, New York: Reader's Digest, 1977). Information about word origins has been gleaned from this book and similar works on etymology.
4. Augustine, *The City of God*, book IV, chapters 16-24.
5. William Smith, *A Dictionary of the Bible* (Grand Rapids: Zondervan Publishing House, 1948), article: "Easter."
6. Madeleine Miller and J. Lane Miller, *Harper's Bible Dictionary* (New York: Harper and Brothers, 1959 edition), article: "English Bible."
7. *The Jewish Encyclopedia* (New York: Funk and Wagnall, 1901), articles: "Calendar," and "Calendar, History of."
8. *Ibid*, p. 500.
9. Alexander Hislop, *The Two Babylons* (Neptune, New Jersey: Loizeaux Brothers), p. 104.
10. Austen Henry Layard, *Nineveh and Babylon* (London, 1853), pp. 92, 93.
11. Hastings' *Encyclopedia of Religion and Ethics* (New York: Charles Scribner Sons, 1928) article: "Festivals and Fasts."
12. Hartman, *op. cit.*, p. 71.
13. *The Catholic Encyclopedia* (New York: Robert Appleton Company, 1907) article: "Easter."
14. James Hasting, *Hastings' Dictionary of the Bible* (New York: Charles Scribner's Sons, 1909), article: "Games."

15. Charles Panati, *The Browser's Book of Beginnings* (Boston: Houghton Mifflin, 1984), p. 376.
16. R. Laird Harris, *Theological Wordbook of the Old Testament* (Chicago: Moody Press, 1980), Vol. 2, p. 972.
17. *The World Book Encyclopedia* (Chicago: World Book, Inc., 1991), article: "Easter."
18. "Heavenly Sunshine," George H. Cook, 1899.
19. "There is Sunshine in My Soul Today," John R. Sweney, 1887.
20. *Harper's Bible Dictionary, op. cit.*, article: "Moon."
21. *The Jewish Encyclopedia, op. cit.*, articles: "Shovriot" and "Sukkah."
22. David Wallechinsky and Irving Wallace, *The People's Almanac* (Garden City, New York: Doubleday, 1975), pp. 939, 940.
23. Catherine B. Avery, editor, *The New Century Classical Handbook* (New York: Appleton-Century-Crofts, Inc.), p. 345.

Companion books to *EASTER, IS IT PAGAN?*
by Ralph Woodrow

THREE DAYS AND THREE NIGHTS —RECONSIDERED

Of special interest to Christians who hold the Wednesday/Saturday view regarding Christ's burial and resurrection—reasons why this view should be reconsidered. Why do *20* verses use the term "in three days" or "the third day," and only *one* "three days and three nights"? If it was late on the sabbath when the women found the tomb empty and saw the resurrected Christ, as some teach, why would they be taking spices to the tomb the next morning? (64 pages).

CHRISTMAS—RECONSIDERED

Is Christmas an ancient pagan festival to which the name of Christ has been falsely attached? Does "mas" in the word "Christmas" give it a Roman Catholic meaning? Shepherds did not "abide in the fields" in winter—*or did they?* Are birthday celebrations "pagan"? Did Jeremiah condemn Christmas trees? (64 pages)

THE BABYLON CONNECTION?

Shows that claims about Babylonian origins often lack connection, takes a closer look at the oft-quoted *The Two Babylons* by Hislop. Was Nimrod a deformed, ugly black man, married to a beautiful white woman named Semiramis? Are candles, black clergy garments, the cross symbol, papal mitre, halos, I.H.S., round wafers, and church steeples of pagan origin? (128 pages).

For a catalog and ordering information, please contact:

RALPH WOODROW
P.O. BOX 21
PALM SPRINGS, CA 92263-0021

Phone order line: (760) 323-9882
Fax: (760) 323-3982

Ralph and Arlene Woodrow

Ralph has had the opportunity to speak for many different churches, groups, and conferences over the years, sharing the glad news of Jesus Christ. He has sought to accept Biblical truths, regardless of which group may or may not teach those truths, but always "searching the scriptures to see if those things are so."

Arlene has had the opportunity to speak and share in various women's ministries, Bible studies, and as Bible college instructor. Her singing and musical abilites have provided an added dimension. She also is a Christian writer.

Books published by the Woodrow ministry number about 500,000 copies in print.